Your Amazing Itty Bitty® Grief Book

15 Chapters on How to Support Family and Friends on Their Journey

Do you ever find yourself at a loss for words when you know someone whose loved one(s) have passed? Do you avoid talking about what a person might be grieving about, or avoid them altogether because they are grieving?

In this Itty Bitty Book you will be given:

- the tools to comfort and support family and friends during a time of loss,

- the ability to hold the space for someone to grieve in silence,

- and the knowledge to stay away from clichés that can be hurtful without meaning to be i.e. "Everything happens for a reason."

If you or someone you know is grieving, as we all will be doing at sometime in our lives, then this Itty Bitty® book is a must read.

Your Amazing Itty Bitty® Grief Book

15 Chapters on How to Support Family and Friends on Their Journey

Lisa Y. Herrington

Published by Itty Bitty® Publishing
A subsidiary of S & P Productions, Inc.

Copyright © 2020 **Lisa Y. Herrington**

Printed in the United States of America

Itty Bitty Publishing
311 Main Street, Suite D
El Segundo, CA 90245
(310) 640-8885

ISBN: 978-1-950326-47-1

This book is dedicated to Brady Randolph, one of my twin sons, who lived less than 24 hours. Just enough time to hold him, kiss him, memorize him and fall deeply in love with him before having to say goodbye. Only on earth for a brief moment, my firstborn taught me a lifetime of lessons on grief, grit, gratitude and finding the balance between the sadness and joy of life.

Stop by our Itty Bitty® website Directory to find interesting information on coping with grief from our experts.

www.IttyBittyPublishing.com

Or visit Lisa Herrington at:

https://www.instagram.com/lisaherrington/

Table of Contents

Introduction

Step 1. Show Up

Step 2. Make a Meal

Step 3. Avoid Clichés

Step 4. Say the Deceased's Name

Step 5. Write Down and Remember
Important Dates

Step 6. Don't Compare Grief

Step 7. Do Instead of Ask

Step 8. There is No Reason

Step 9. Be Cautious with Religion

Step 10. Don't Know What to Say; Say
Something

Step 11. Volunteer or Donate

Step 12. Share a Memory

Step 13. Time Doesn't Heal All

Step 14. Be Grateful

Step 15. Lead with Empathy

Introduction

This book is intended to help those at a loss for words when a family member or friend is grieving. Lord knows there were plenty of well-meaning people who wanted to comfort me after losing my son Brady, but had absolutely no idea what to do or say. Hopefully this book will empower readers with tools to help comfort family and friends who are grieving.

Etiquette 1
Show Up

In this Itty Bitty Book, you will find tips on what to say, what not to say, what to do and what not to do when someone you know is grieving.

1. When someone you know is grieving, it is often difficult to know what to say or do.
2. The fear of saying or doing something that might upset the person grieving can paralyze you into not saying or doing anything at all.
3. The absolute worst thing you can do when a person is grieving is to avoid all conversations surrounding the person's loss.
4. The absolute best thing you can do when you don't know what to say or do is to show up. Showing up doesn't have to be physically; it can be through a phone call, a text, an e-mail or good old snail mail.

Show Up Again and Again and Again

While it's important to reach out immediately to someone who has suffered a tragedy; it is crucial to follow-up with the person grieving after the first six weeks.

- The first stages of grief can feel so surreal to all involved. You along with countless others are trying to ease the pain of the loss through calls, texts, cards, meal trains, etc.
- The person grieving is living in a state of shock, denial, sadness, etc. while also likely occupied with the aftermath of the tragedy such as funeral arrangements.
- Once the chaos of the first six weeks is over, it can feel very lonely for the bereaved. They will feel a void with the person tragically missing from their life as well as in the lack of people still checking in to see if they are okay (they're not).
- It is in the weeks and months after someone dies, that it is most important to check in on those directly affected by the loss of a loved one.

Etiquette 2
Make A Meal

Showing up for someone who is grieving can also take the form of a meal made (or delivered) with love. Setting up a meal delivery calendar (ex: Meal Train) is a great way to involve friends and family in an act of kindness for the person(s) grieving.

1. There is a reason food is often referred to as comfort food. Good food, especially home cooked meals can provide a sense of comfort and positivity to a person who is grieving.
2. While there is not much you can do to control the situation when a person is grieving, you can provide comfort and thoughtfulness through a meal.
3. Have no fear if the meal goes uneaten because the person grieving may have no appetite. It's the thought that counts.
4. If you choose to personally drop-off the meal, it will provide you with a great opportunity to talk with the person grieving, listen empathetically and offer a hug. Food can be the gateway to a grieving heart.

Meals and Thoughtful Gestures

Don't fret if you're not a cook, there are plenty of other thoughtful gestures for someone who is grieving. Below are a few to get you thinking in the right direction.

- There are countless delivery services that provide meals and won't require you to lift a finger in the kitchen.
- A massage or spa gift certificate is a nice gesture you may give someone who is grieving to promote self-care.
- You may gift a person a piece of clothing, artwork or jewelry to uplift their spirits. Bonus points if the gift has sentimental value (i.e. a bracelet with the initials of the person who has passed).
- A handwritten note is one of the simplest, most personal gestures to let a person know you are thinking of them.
- Make a donation or volunteer in honor of the person who has died.

Etiquette 3
Avoid Cliché Sayings

Cliché Sayings can be helpful or harmful depending on the thoughts and beliefs of someone who is grieving. If you choose to reference them, be selective and thoughtful when using them. Below are several clichés that should be avoided.

1. "Everything Happens for A Reason." Death doesn't always make sense and when someone dies it is often hard for the bereaved to find reasoning or meaning in the loss especially if the death happens outside the natural order of a lifespan.
2. "I can't imagine what you're going through." Grief is a very lonely feeling. Telling the bereaved you can't imagine what they are going through, may heighten feelings of isolation; as if no one can relate to their feelings of sadness.
3. "At least you have…" There is no replacement for a person who died. There is no need to point out what the bereaved still has. Allow them to mourn for what they no longer have.
4. "They are in a better place now." Most often a bereaved friend or family member would argue the best place for their lost loved one is on earth, right beside them.

What to Say Instead of a Cliché

When someone dies it can be hard to find the right words to say. Sometimes there are no right words to say. Rather than referencing a cliché, do this instead:

- Hug the bereaved.
- Tell them you are sorry for their loss.
- Listen with empathy and non-judgment.
- Check in periodically.
- Let them know you are thinking of them and the deceased.

Etiquette 4
Say the Deceased's Name

Death is an uncomfortable topic for many, especially when death falls out of a normal life cycle. Such is the case with deaths that involve young people or are tragic, unexpected or unexplained in nature. It's a common misconception that when death is acknowledged, it triggers painful memories for those most affected by the loss. Contrary to this belief, when someone dies they are on the minds of the bereaved more often than not and for them to know that others are thinking of the deceased can be incredibly comforting. You will not remind someone of their pain by speaking the name of a loved one who has passed; you will only validate they were here and they are remembered.

1. One day, six weeks, six months, six years, sixty years...always speak the names of those that have gone before you.
2. Even better write their names down, in a thoughtful note. Simple gestures can feel like gigantic hugs to someone who has suffered great loss.
3. The greatest gift you can give someone grieving is to not let the memory of their loved one die too.

Don't be Scared to Say the Name of the Loved One

Saying the name of a person who died to a loved one is a sign of acknowledgment that you recognize the life of the person who has passed. We talk about the living all the time; we should not be scared to mention those who died.

- Speaking the name of someone who has passed will help keep the individual's spirit alive and present amongst the bereaved.
- Saying the name of the deceased to the people who love them most is like wrapping the bereaved in an enormously comforting blanket.
- Unprompted remembrances of the loved one who has passed can be a beautiful gift to the bereaved.

Etiquette 5
Write Down and Remember
Important Dates

The day someone dies is just as important as the day someone is born. Include dates of death on your calendar so when that date rolls around, you can reach out and let loved ones know you are thinking about them.

1. Birthdates are universal celebrations displayed on the calendars. Death dates should be as well.
2. If you are not comfortable writing the date of someone's death on your calendar, pick a symbol. An example would be to draw a flower or cross next to the person's name that passed on the date they died.

Acknowledging Important Dates

The first step is to write down important dates and the most important step is to do something thoughtful on those dates.

- Send a card, text or make a phone call to acknowledge the date that someone passed.
- Schedule a lunch date, spa day, walk or long phone conversation on the date of passing.
- Distractions are a great way to occupy someone who is grieving. While they will still feel hurt and sorrow, they will inevitably appreciate the recognition of a painful anniversary often overlooked.

Etiquette 6
Don't Compare Grief

Grief is very personal. Humans will inevitably suffer loss. Grief is the product of loss and the way grief is felt, handled and rationalized is relative to past experiences. The last thing a person who is heavily grieving wants to hear is how your loss(es) are better or worse than theirs.

1. Don't compare hurt. It's all painful.
2. Rather than comparing losses, it's best to sit and listen to the person grieving. Let them talk about the person they loved and lost, listen and empathize but don't compare.

Grief Craves Empathy

When someone is grieving they need support, encouragement, patience from others and above all else empathy.

- Grief can be very lonely.
- When someone is grieving they may feel like they are in a boat navigating enormous waves all alone.
- Empathizing with grief rather than comparing or shying away from grief can help those suffering begin to pick up the broken pieces.
- It is okay to share your loss with someone who is grieving, but don't allow your loss to overshadow their loss.
- Never, ever tell someone you couldn't imagine going through what they went through. Instead explain, while you may not fully understand, you will support them though their journey.
- People don't expect, nor would they want you to know what their loss feels like. They want you to stand beside them, support them and show them you care about their loss.

Etiquette 7
Do Instead of Ask

"Let me know if there is anything I can do for you." While this is a kind gesture, it's not something you want to say to someone grieving. They likely don't know what they need or what can be done for them because all they want is the person who died back. Grieving is extremely exhausting and it's hard to find the energy to let others know how to help during hard times. The best thing to do is take action and do things for the bereaved that you believe would make life easier for them.

1. Do what feels good and right for someone who is grieving.
2. If you are unsure of what to do, simply send a text to let the person know you are thinking of them.

Things to do for Someone Grieving

Below is a list of kind gestures to show someone who is grieving that you care:

- Make dinner
- Set up a meal delivery service
- Set up a donation site for the family (ex: Go Fund Me) if a financial burden has been created due to the loss. Make sure to get their okay on this first.
- Schedule an outing for the bereaved
- Send flowers
- Write a card
- Donate to a cause to honor the deceased

Etiquette 8
There is No Reason

When someone dies, especially tragically or really young, it's human nature to want to search for reason, but don't do it. The last thing a person who lost someone near and dear wants to hear is that their loved one died for a reason. It's easy to rationalize losing a job when a door opens for a better one or surviving a breakup only to find the love of your life, but it is not easy (nor should it be done) to try and rationalize death. Death doesn't happen for a reason, but the people most affected by the death have the power to find reason and meaning in the loss.

1. After a death, it can often take time (years) for those grieving the death to see the light after loss.
2. Light after loss can take on many forms; possibly more children, a memorial foundation set-up in honor of the deceased that betters the world, tribute books and art, connecting with others that understand, and the list goes on.
3. While there is no replacing a loved one, blessings abound to those who have lost, once they are open to receiving them.

Do Not Rationalize Death to Someone Grieving

There is no rationalizing death. When we try to find a reason for death we are ultimately searching for an answer as to why the person had to die. If we can answer the question why someone had to die, we feel like we have more control of the situation. Truth be told, no one has control of death and trying to rationalize death to someone who is deeply hurting can be painful. There is likely no reason good enough to ease the pain of acute grief that happens soon after losing a loved one.

- There are no good reasons for death.
- Regardless of the nature of the loss, it is hard to find meaning.
- Best to not search for the meaning of death.
- Meaning and reason in loss can be found by the bereaved, but may take months or years, and must come from within.
- Grief is a process and everyone grieves differently. It's okay to lend support, but don't force any beliefs on the bereaved. Instead allow them to explore what paths help them heal the most.

Step 9
Tread Lightly with Religion

We all come from different backgrounds, cultures, religions and beliefs. After a person loses a loved one, religion may be a source of strength and a beacon of light. The loss may also cause the bereaved to question everything about religion and beliefs prior to the loss. In either instance, allow the person grieving to explore their new relationship with religion and spirituality (whether they choose to have one or not) without any judgment or fear of criticism.

1. Religion and spirituality are a personal choice.
2. Without judgment, allow the bereaved space to explore their new relationship with religion and spirituality after loss.

Non-judgmental Support is Important

- Religion and spirituality may be in question by someone who has experienced loss.
- Religion and spirituality may be embraced by someone who has experienced a loss.
- Religion may be left behind by someone who has experienced a loss.
- All of the above are okay.
- Support the bereaved no matter what their religious decisions are after a loss.

Etiquette 10
Don't Know What to Say; Say Something

There is a fear that if the bereaved is reminded of their loss in a conversation, this will invoke sadness. Contrary to this belief, hearing the name of, or a memory about their loved one may elicit positive feelings.

1. Say the name of the person who died to their loved ones.
2. Share a memory about the person who died.
3. Don't be afraid to share a funny memory. Laughter is okay when someone is grieving.
4. If what you say evokes uncomfortable emotions, that's okay. Hold this uncomfortable space with them.

Saying Something is Better Than Saying Nothing.

- Acknowledge the loss.
- Pick up the phone. Drop-in for a visit.
- Tell the bereaved you are very sorry for their loss.
- Let the bereaved know you are thinking about them.
- If you can't find the right words, write them down. Send a text or write your thoughts in a card.

Step 11
Volunteer or Donate

There are many opportunities to volunteer for an organization or donate in honor of someone who has passed away. This act of kindness can mean so much to the bereaved.

1. Volunteering or making a donation are great ways to support the bereaved while honoring the loss.
2. Encouraging others to volunteer or donate gives them direction on how to lend their support.
3. Participate in a benefit walk, run, ride, or challenge in honor of the person who has passed,
4. As always, it's the thought that counts the most.

Find the Right Organization for the Cause

If you don't know where to volunteer or donate, ask the bereaved family for suggestions. Below are a few ways to get involved.

- Organized walk/runs
- Benefit concerts
- Foundations
- Charitable causes aligned with the mission of the person who died (or the mission of the bereaved).
- Support group

These are just a few examples of the many ways you can volunteer or donate to a great cause while supporting a bereaved friend or family member

Step 12
Share a Memory (Bonus Points for an Unprompted Memory)

As time passes, the bereaved may become fearful that their loved one who has died will be forgotten. Life resumes as normal for everyone else but for the bereaved it may stand still for a long time. Hearing a family member or friend share an unprompted memory about the person who died is welcome and appreciated. Often it signifies to the bereaved that their loved one has not been forgotten.

1. Memories, journals, mementos, photos, stories, memorial events, next of kin, etc. are the legacies that those who die leave behind.
2. Having the courage to bring up a memory, point out a photo, share a special story (might even be a funny one) allows the bereaved to do the same in a comfortable, non-judgmental space.
3. Bringing up the person's name, sharing memories or acknowledging their birth date or the date of loss is important and appreciated.

Don't Allow Memories to Die

When someone dies very young, there are often few or no memories to share. Remember to bring up the person's name, date of birth and date of passing. This all rings true for any loss.

- Telling the bereaved you are thinking of their loved one helps lessen the fear the person who died will be forgotten.
- Sharing memories allows the bereaved to feel comfortable doing the same.
- Swapping memories keeps legacies alive.

Etiquette 13
Time Doesn't Heal All

Time may lessen the intense pain that grief initially causes, but it doesn't heal all. Grief is a visceral reaction to loss and can look and feel very different for everyone. During the first weeks and months after a loss occurs, grief may be very intense (often referred to as acute grief). There are different phases of grief and the severity of each are unique to the bereaved and the loss they have endured. Shock, sadness, anger, jealousy, guilt, disbelief and acceptance are common phases of grief. Depending on how they grieve, the bereaved can remain in each stage for an unspecified amount of time. It is important to be patient and support the bereaved through each stage of grief. Let them experience each stage, feel each emotion and learn to live in this new space - their "new normal."

1. There are different stages of grief and an unspecified amount of time it will take to move through each stage.
2. Allow the bereaved time in each stage to feel, process and evolve.
3. Time doesn't heal all, but it does soften the grief.

The New Normal

The loss cannot be undone so the bereaved must learn to live without the person who has passed away. This is their new normal.

- Time will allow the bereaved to feel more comfortable in their new normal.
- Be patient with the bereaved and the multitude of emotions that various stages of grief may evoke.
- Time does not heal, but it does help soften the grief. Unwavering support from family and friends is a must.

Etiquette 14
Be Grateful

Life is precious. Life is fragile. Life is beautiful. Life is sad. Life is wonderful. Be grateful for the ability to laugh, play, love, hurt, cry, breathe, everything and anything that makes us human. It's not always easy for someone who has suffered a loss to watch others take life for granted. Loss may cause the bereaved to feel a heightened sense of mortality, thus a greater appreciation for life. While it may be hard to understand this depending on your circumstances, do your best to empathize.

1. Be grateful for life. Each moment is a gift.
2. Bereaved individuals may have a heightened sense of mortality and/or a greater appreciation for life. Support them in this space.

Gratitude Prompts

Below are tips for living a gratitude-filled life:

- Every morning write down 3-5 things you are grateful for.
- Say them out loud.
- Repeat this exercise every morning.
- Notice how your gratitude list changes and evolves.
- Read a gratitude-filled book.
- Gift the book to a friend.
- Perform random acts of kindness.
- Exercise to feel better.
- Spend time outside to experience the beauty of nature.
- Smile. Smile. Smile.

Etiquette 15
Lead with Empathy

Sympathy is feeling compassion or pity for the hardships and losses one suffers. Empathy is the ability to understand and share the feelings of another. While it is important to sympathize and feel compassion for the bereaved, it can be more important to put yourself in the shoes of a family member suffering. To understand that grief is hard, it's emotional and the journey through it may require much time and energy. Empathizing with those who are bereaved and having the ability to walk beside them, offering a pillar of support as they navigate uncharted territory is incredibly important.

1. Empathy helps family and friends understand how those who have suffered loss feel; enabling them to respond appropriately when discussing the loss.
2. Family and friends who demonstrate empathy can help the bereaved not feel so alone.

Demonstrating Empathy

Below are ways to effectively demonstrate empathy:

- Active listening. Listen with purpose and without distractions such as phones or thoughts about your to-do list.
- Make eye contact while communicating.
- Open up. Sharing vulnerabilities helps form an emotional connection.
- Withhold judgment.
- Offer physical affection such as a hug or an arm around the shoulder.
- Offer help big or small.
- Continue to show up long after the loss to support and check-in on the bereaved.
- Show kindness, compassion, patience, love to everyone and a little extra to those grieving.

You've finished. Before you go...

Tweet/share that you finished this book.

Please star rate this book.

Reviews are solid gold to writers. Please take a few minutes to give us some Itty Bitty feedback.

ABOUT THE AUTHOR

Lisa Yackzan Herrington is a mom to four beautiful children on earth and one in Heaven. She is a daughter, sister, wife, friend, business owner and fitness enthusiast. She owns a fitness studio, FIT House, in northern California and spends her days teaching a plethora of fitness classes and training amazing clients. After losing her first born (a twin) she realized how important exercise was not just for the physical body, but for the mind. She often refers to her line of work as movement therapy; an act that strengthens the body, mind and soul. When Lisa is not on the fitness room floor, she can be found driving her kids to and from various activities, volunteering, running while listening to her favorite podcasts, writing, hanging with her family and friends and vacationing near the water. She enjoys waterskiing, snow-skiing, the ocean, baking, a good Cabernet or micro-brew and making genuine connections with people. Lisa manages the Brady Randolph Herrington Community Foundation which was set-up in honor of her son. Each year on their birthday, Brady's twin brother Luke, decides where a portion of the money is donated. It's acts of kindness like this that bring beauty to tragic situations. Lisa wrote this book with the intention to help family and friends support their loved ones through grief. She is eternally grateful to everyone who continues to support her family and keep her son's memory alive.

If you enjoyed this Itty Bitty® book you might also like…

- **Your Amazing Itty Bitty® Gratitude Book** – Belinda Lee Cook

- **Your Amazing Itty Bitty® Stress Reduction Book** – Denise Thomson, CHC

- **Your Amazing Itty Bitty® Affirmations Book** – Micaela Passeri

Or any of the many Amazing Itty Bitty® books available on line at www.ittybittypublishing.com

Made in the USA
Columbia, SC
10 October 2020